As a graphic designer who loves to color,
I am thrilled to combine my two passions
in the pages of this coloring book.

Coloring allows me to explore my creative side
and experiment with all manner of materials
to create unique pieces of art.

I hope you create your latest
piece of art within the pages of my book.
I look forward to seeing all of your colored pages!
Post them on my website at
www.facebook.com/beckytorresdesigns.
Enjoy!

Note:
Markers and gel pens may bleed through paper. Please place a blank piece of paper behind the page you are coloring. Several are included at the end of the book.

© Copyright Becky Torres Designs   www.facebook.com/BeckyTorresDesigns

See all of the coloring books by
Becky Torres Designs
at
www.amazon.com/author/beckytorresdesigns

Copyright

Copyright ©2016 by Becky Torres Designs. All rights reserved.

This book may not be reproduced in whole or in part, in any form or by any means, electronic or mechanical, including photocopying, recording, or by any information storage and retrieval system now known or hereafter invented, without written permission from the publisher.

Designed by Becky Torres
with additional material adapted from www.freepix.com.

Becky Torres Designs
Charlotte, NC 28227   USA
www.facebook.com/beckytorresdesigns

© Copyright Becky Torres Designs   www.facebook.com/BeckyTorresDesigns

© Copyright Becky Torres Designs   www.facebook.com/beckytorresdesigns

© Copyright Becky Torres Designs   www.facebook.com/beckytorresdesigns

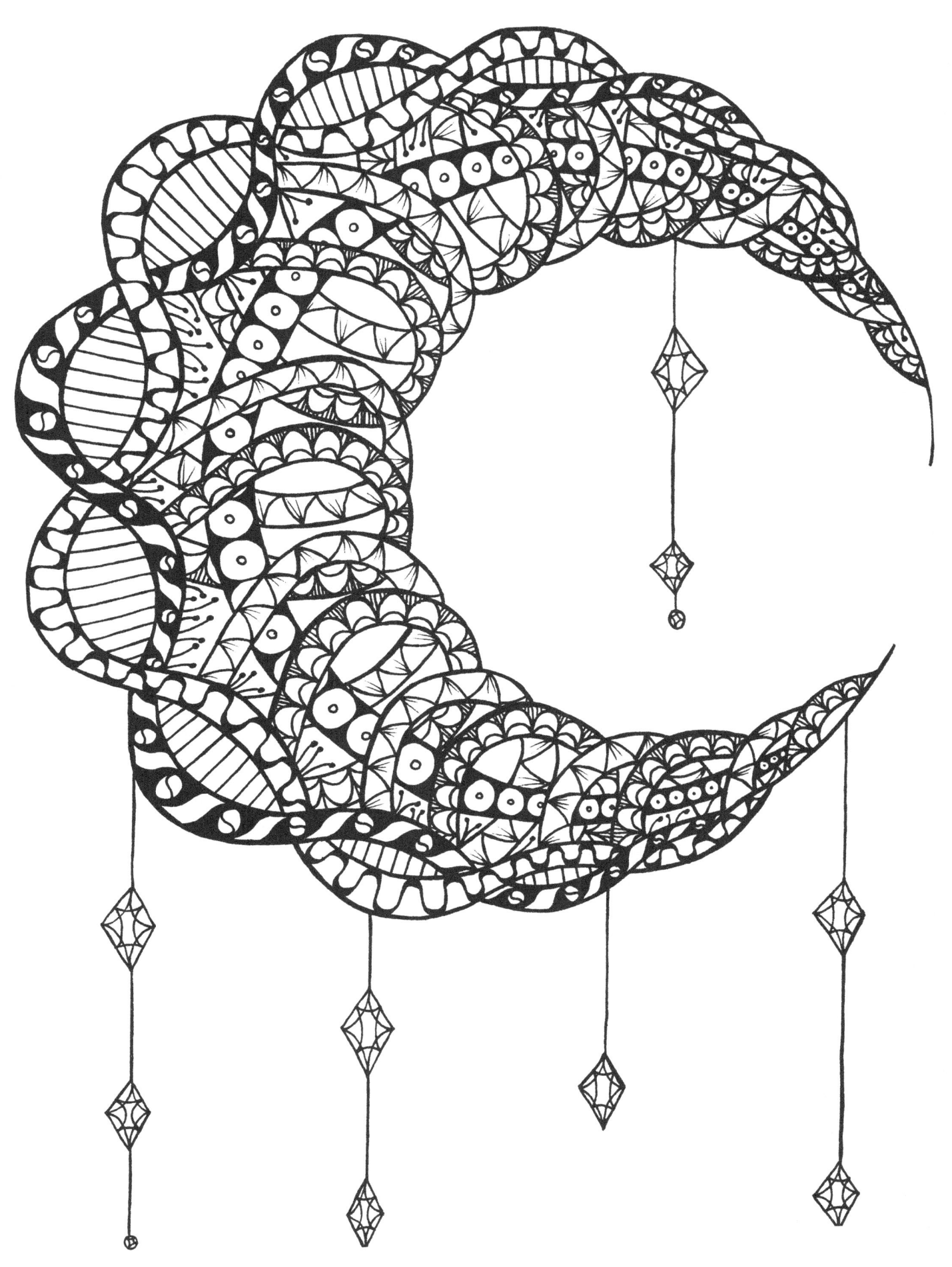

©Copyright Becky Torres Designs   www.facebook.com/beckytorresdesigns

© Copyright Becky Torres Designs   www.facebook.com/BeckyTorresDesigns

© Copyright Becky Torres Designs   www.facebook.com/beckytorresdesigns

© Copyright Becky Torres Designs   www.facebook.com/BeckyTorresDesigns

© Copyright Becky Torres Designs   www.facebook.com/beckytorresdesigns

© Copyright Becky Torres Designs   www.facebook.com/BeckyTorresDesigns

©Copyright Becky Torres Designs   www.facebook.com/beckytorresdesigns

© Copyright Becky Torres Designs www.facebook.com/BeckyTorresDesigns

©Copyright Becky Torres Designs   www.facebook.com/beckytorresdesigns

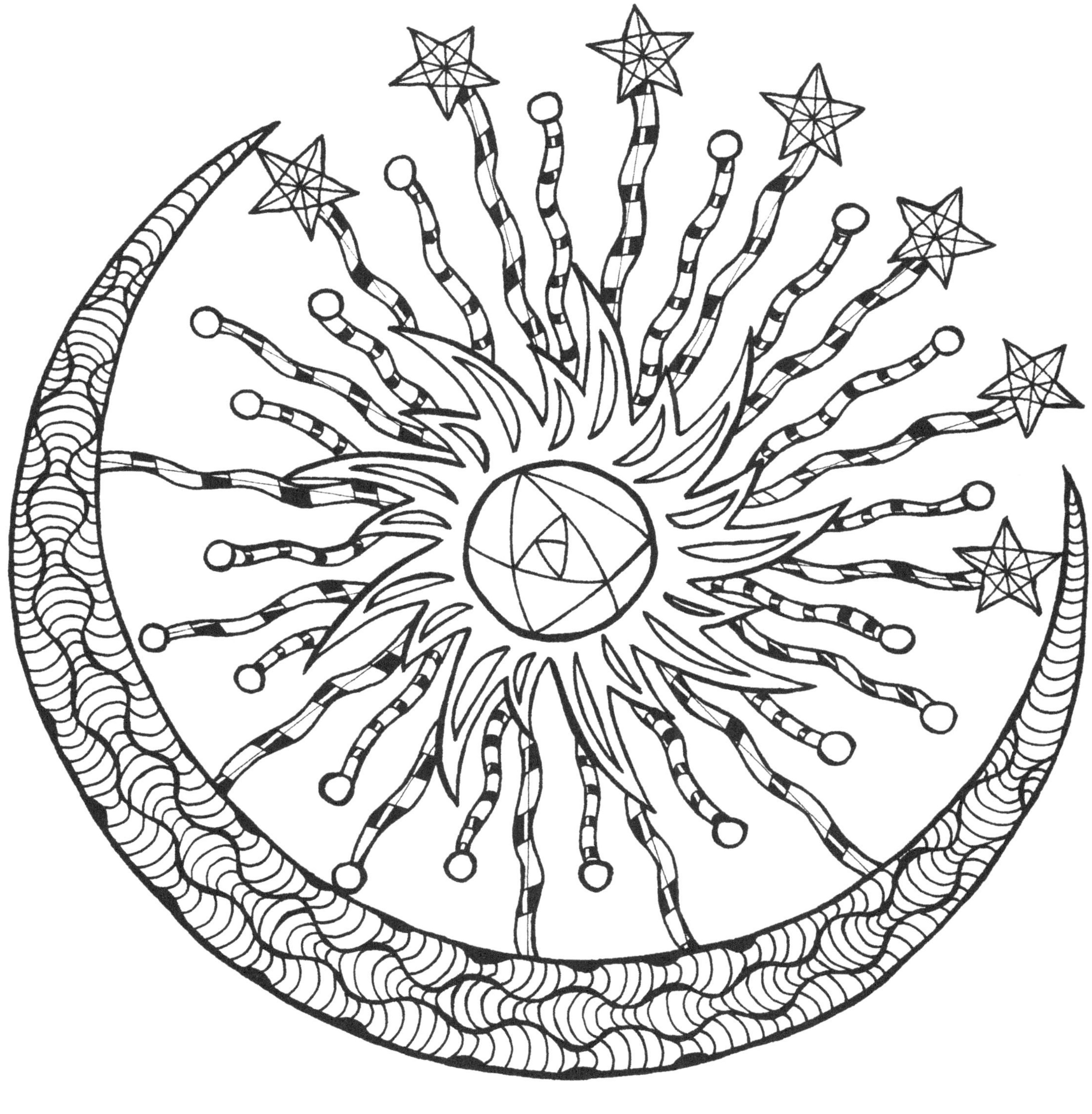

©Copyright Becky Torres Designs   www.facebook.com/beckytorresdesigns

© Copyright Becky Torres Designs   www.facebook.com/BeckyTorresDesigns

©Copyright Becky Torres Designs   www.facebook.com/beckytorresdesigns

© Copyright Becky Torres Designs   www.facebook.com/beckytorresdesigns

©Copyright Becky Torres Designs   www.facebook.com/beckytorresdesigns

©Copyright Becky Torres Designs   www.facebook.com/beckytorresdesigns

©Copyright Becky Torres Designs   www.facebook.com/beckytorresdesigns

© Copyright Becky Torres Designs   www.facebook.com/BeckyTorresDesigns

©Copyright Becky Torres Designs   www.facebook.com/beckytorresdesigns

© Copyright Becky Torres Designs   www.facebook.com/beckytorresdesigns

© Copyright Becky Torres Designs   www.facebook.com/beckytorresdesigns

© Copyright Becky Torres Designs   www.facebook.com/BeckyTorresDesigns

© Copyright Becky Torres Designs   www.facebook.com/beckytorresdesigns

Copyright Becky Torres Designs   www.facebook.com/BeckyTorresDesigns

©Copyright Becky Torres Designs   www.facebook.com/beckytorresdesigns

© Copyright Becky Torres Designs   www.facebook.com/beckytorresdesigns

© Copyright Becky Torres Designs   www.facebook.com/beckytorresdesigns

© Copyright BeckyTorres Designs   www.facebook.com/BeckyTorresDesigns

© Copyright Becky Torres Designs   www.facebook.com/beckytorresdesigns

© Copyright Becky Torres Designs   www.facebook.com/beckytorresdesigns

©Copyright Becky Torres Designs   www.facebook.com/beckytorresdesigns

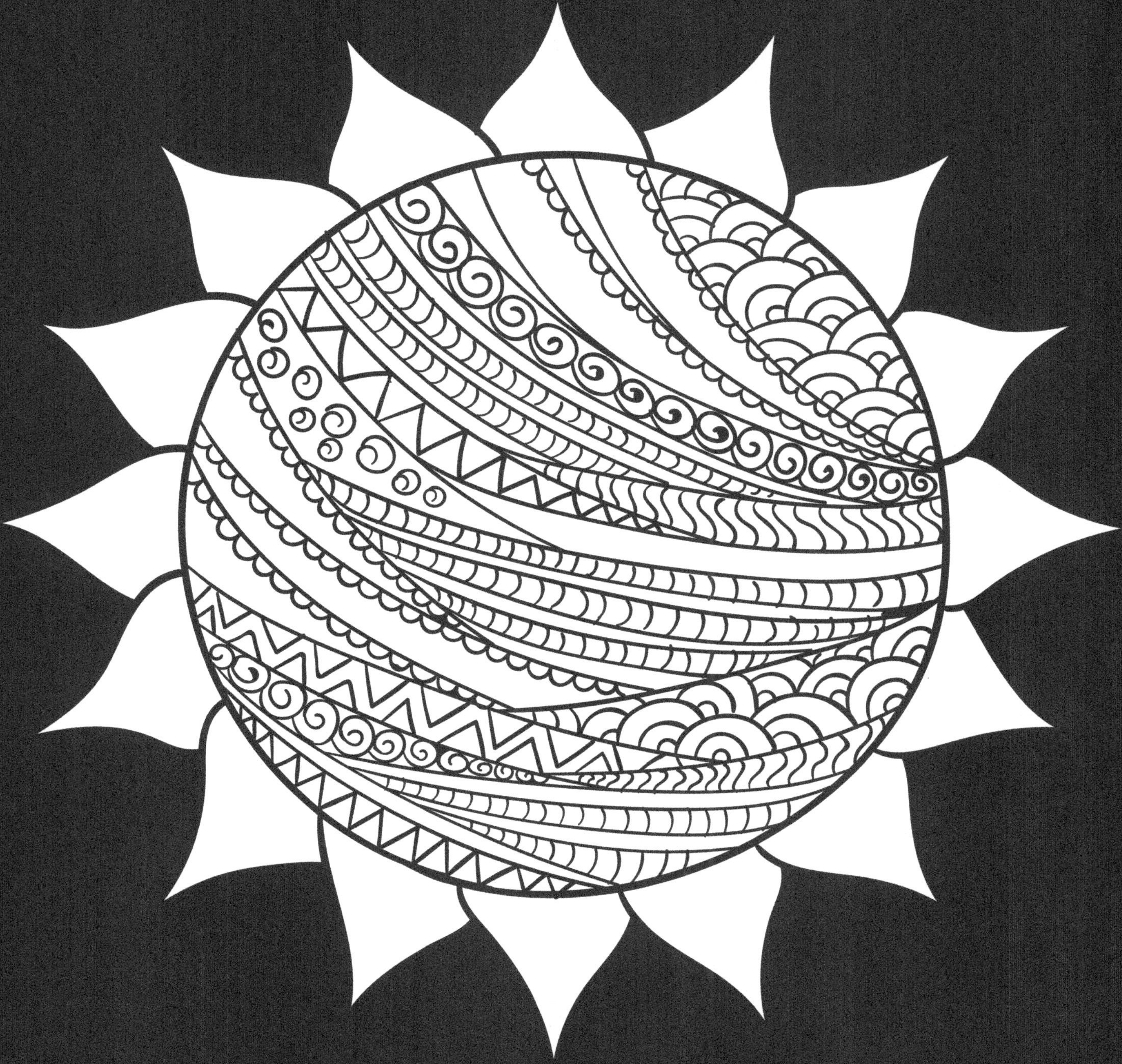

©Copyright Becky Torres Designs   www.facebook.com/beckytorresdesigns

© Copyright Becky Torres Designs   www.facebook.com/beckytorresdesigns

©Copyright Becky Torres Designs   www.facebook.com/beckytorresdesigns

© Copyright Becky Torres Designs   www.facebook.com/BeckyTorresDesigns

© Copyright Becky Torres Designs   www.facebook.com/beckytorresdesigns

© Copyright Becky Torres Designs   www.facebook.com/beckytorresdesigns

© Copyright Becky Torres Designs   www.facebook.com/beckytorresdesigns

© Copyright Becky Torres Designs   www.facebook.com/beckytorresdesigns

© Copyright Becky Torres Designs   www.facebook.com/beckytorresdesigns

© Copyright Becky Torres Designs   www.facebook.com/BeckyTorresDesigns

© Copyright Becky Torres Designs   www.facebook.com/beckytorresdesigns

© Copyright Becky Torres Designs   www.facebook.com/beckytorresdesigns

© Copyright Becky Torres Designs   www.facebook.com/beckytorresdesigns

© Copyright Becky Torres Designs   www.facebook.com/beckytorresdesigns

© Copyright Becky Torres Designs   www.facebook.com/beckytorresdesigns

© Copyright Becky Torres Designs   www.facebook.com/beckytorresdesigns

© Copyright Becky Torres Designs   www.facebook.com/beckytorresdesigns

© Copyright Becky Torres Designs   www.facebook.com/beckytorresdesigns

© Copyright Becky Torres Designs   www.facebook.com/beckytorresdesigns

©Copyright Becky Torres Designs   www.facebook.com/beckytorresdesigns

©Copyright Becky Torres Designs   www.facebook.com/beckytorresdesigns

Made in the USA
Columbia, SC
04 December 2023